GROSS UNIVERSE

Your Guide to All
Disgusting
Things Under the Sun

written by
JEFF SZPIRGLAS

illustrated by
MICHAEL CHO

MAPLE
TREE
PRESS

Maple Tree Press Inc.
51 Front Street East, Suite 200, Toronto, Ontario M5E 1B3
www.mapletreepress.com

Distributed in Canada by Raincoast Books
9050 Shaughnessy Street, Vancouver, British Columbia V6P 6E5

Distributed in the United States by Publishers Group West
1700 Fourth Street, Berkeley, California 94710

Dedication
In loving memory of my appendix, 1976–1988
–JS

Cataloguing in Publication Data
Szpirglas, Jeff
    Gross universe : your guide to all disgusting things under
the sun / written by Jeff Szpirglas ; illustrated by Michael Cho.

Includes index.
ISBN-13: 978-1-897066-63-8 (bound) / ISBN-10: 1-897066-63-5 (bound)
ISBN-13: 978-1-897066-39-3 (pbk.) / ISBN-10: 1-897066-39-2 (pbk.)

    1. Physiology—Juvenile literature. 2. Human physiology—
Juvenile literature. 3. Parasites—Juvenile literature. I. Cho,
Michael II. Title.

QP37.S996 2006   j573   C2004-904629-2

Design & art direction: Claudia Dávila
Illustrations: Michael Cho

We acknowledge the financial support of the Canada Council for the Arts, the Ontario
Arts Council, the Government of Canada through the Book Publishing Industry
Development Program (BPIDP), and the Government of Ontario through the Ontario
Media Development Corporation's Book Initiative for our publishing activities.

ONTARIO ARTS COUNCIL
CONSEIL DES ARTS DE L'ONTARIO

Printed in Hong Kong

B   C   D   E   F

CONTENTS

Extreme close-up of what you—yes, you!—are shedding onto these pristine pages.

A Note to the Reader

The coolest pet I ever owned was a brown snake. I was ten years old and obsessed with reptiles. Snakes, lizards, crocodilians, you name it: any creature covered in scales was as good as it got. So you can imagine my joy when I finally had one living in a terrarium in my room.

My mom hated the snake. She couldn't walk into my room without seeing the terrarium and shuddering. What was her problem? The snake was a sleek, elegant piece of nature. It blended into its surroundings perfectly. It was an efficient hunter of slugs. And I only let it hunt Mom once.

Then one day I came home from summer camp to discover close to 30 little baby snakes writhing and squirming in the tank. Their large eyes bugged out of their heads. When my mom came up to announce it was time for dinner, she saw the snakes and nearly fainted.

The book you're about to read is a lot like the snakes that nauseated my mother.

If you're like me, you're going to enjoy reading about flies whose larvae burrow into human skin; baby birds that barf oil at their enemies; or the fossilized poop left by dinosaurs. The world around you is gross. Well, before you feel you're above all that, why don't we take a break and stop to think about you for a moment. Your finger-prints are soiling the book cover, and flakes of your dead skin are raining down all over this page.

Face it, I'm gross. You're gross. And the world we live in? Definitely gross. It's best just to learn as much about it as you can. That way you can disgust your family with these facts at the dinner table.

Bon appétit!

Jeff

5

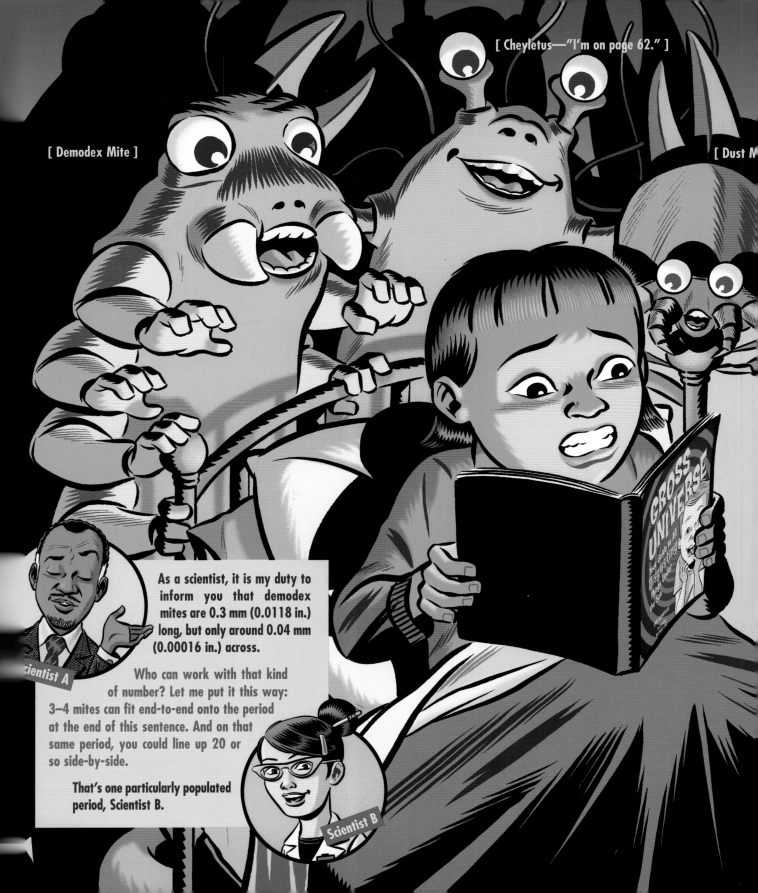

[Demodex Mite]

[Cheyletus—"I'm on page 62."]

[Dust M

As a scientist, it is my duty to inform you that demodex mites are 0.3 mm (0.0118 in.) long, but only around 0.04 mm (0.00016 in.) across.

Who can work with that kind of number? Let me put it this way: 3–4 mites can fit end-to-end onto the period at the end of this sentence. And on that same period, you could line up 20 or so side-by-side.

That's one particularly populated period, Scientist B.

Scientist A

Scientist B

GROSS UNIVERSE

Before We Begin...

A Word About Your Gross Friends

IF YOU THINK YOU'RE GOING TO BE READING THIS BOOK ALONE, THINK AGAIN. LIVING ON AND INSIDE YOUR BODY ARE THOUSANDS OF CREATURES: SOME GOOD, SOME BAD, AND MOST JUST PLAIN UGLY.

It's a Mite, Mite World!

Members of the arachnid class, mites are some of the oldest animals to walk the earth, with a lineage stretching back over 370 million years. But mites don't just walk the earth, they can live in fresh and saltwater, and thrive in deserts and the tropics. Some have even been found in Antarctica, where they survive by producing a chemical that resembles antifreeze.

Demodex Mites

These eight-legged critters are shaped like tiny cigars. Their stubby legs all poke out near their front ends, forcing the mites to drag their long rear ends across your skin at speeds up to 1 cm (less than 1/2 in.) an hour. Demodex mites make themselves at home on your head, in your nose, and even around your eyelashes.

House Dust Mites

There's no point in cowering under a pillow to hide from the dust mites (of which there are dozens of species). That's where dust mites call home! Hordes of these guys live on our pillows, rugs, and mattresses. They thrive in a humid environment—often provided by our warm, moist breath. These flesh-eaters dine on skin that has flaked off our bodies. One healthy dust mite can poop around 20 anal pellets a day. Their pellets get scattered in the air with our movements, which can cause people to suffer from problems including allergies, eczema (a skin inflammation), and asthma.

Don't Forget Bacteria!

Though bacteria make up less than 0.5% of your body weight, there are more bacteria living on you than there are people in the world (a thousand of them alone could fit on the head of a pin). It's been estimated that humans have 50 million individual bacteria per square centimeter (1/2 inch) of skin! Oily, sweaty places like your armpits have many more. But there are some places where you'll find little to no microbial life, like your urine-storing bladder or the lower regions of the lungs. And just so you know, it's been estimated that there are nine times more bacteria in and on the human body than there are cells in the human body!

Sickening Skin

We've already probed the wildlife breeding, living, pooping, and dying on our skin, so why not take a look at ourselves from a new perspective. Why not take a look in the mirror?

(This is a good time to put the book down and do what you're told. A bookmark would be helpful here.)

There. You just stared at one of the largest organs in the animal kingdom. That's right: skin! Now let's zoom in closer. If you could shrink down and explore the surface of your skin, you'd find a seemingly unearthly terrain.

[Hair Follicle]

[Sebaceous Gland]

Skin Is Like...

...a snug-fitting blanket. It's a tough world, and you'll need something to hide under (and to keep your guts from spilling out everywhere). On humans, skin is at its thickest on the soles of your feet and its thinnest on your eyelids.

Skin is like...the ultimate thermos mug. It keeps you cool when it's hot, and it keeps you from losing heat when it's freezing outside.

Best of all, skin is like a layer cake! That's right, it comes in layers: The

The White Stuff

Check out the shoulders on your mom or dad's dark suits. Do you see white specks? If so, please inform them that they have an excess amount of dandruff. Dandruff is the dead skin that flakes off the scalp, becoming dust. So give your parents a good vacuuming and tell them to stop making such a mess.

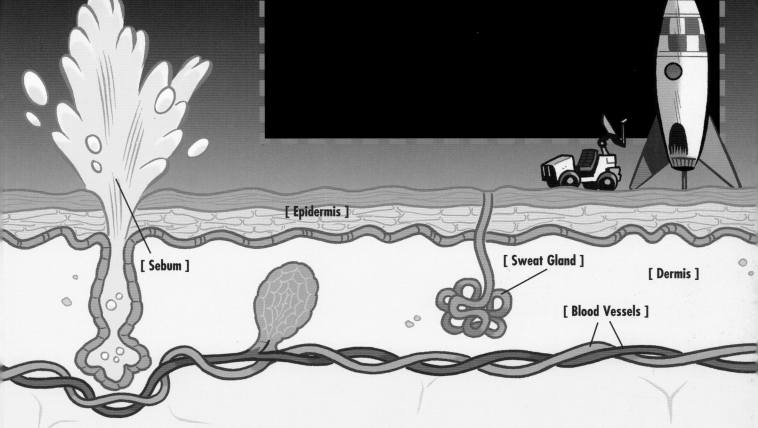

[Epidermis]

[Sebum]

[Sweat Gland]

[Dermis]

[Blood Vessels]

epidermis is the outer layer of your skin. Most of it is made of dead cells that flake off. Underneath, an army of new epidermal cells is waiting to take over. Your skin regenerates itself from top to bottom in around 28 days...JUST LIKE FEBRUARY!

The second layer is the dermis, which is only a little bit easier to say than epidermis. Thicker than the epidermis, the dermis holds sweat and oil glands as well as hair follicles (where hairs sprout from). The sebaceous, or

oil, glands make sebum. Sebum is a greasy substance that covers your body. Yup. You're covered with the stuff. Just try pressing your nose against a window and you'll see for yourself.

[More Sickening Skin]

A Hippo's Red Resin

Consider the skin of the hippopotamus, which is thick and leathery. The epidermis, or outer layer, is quite thin. Hanging around under the hot sun all day would bake the epidermis into crispy chips, which is why hippos tend to stay in the water and mud. And the hippo has another ace up its sleeve. Glands in its skin secrete a sticky red liquid. Some people mistakenly believe that hippos sweat blood, and they're wrong on both counts. The red fluid isn't blood, and it isn't sweat. It's an oily substance (not unlike our human sebum) that coats the animal and keeps it from drying out. Sorry, I have no idea what it tastes like.

Crunchy on the Outside...

And if you thought human skin was out of this world, take a look at the insect kingdom! Unlike mammals, with our bones on the inside and our skin on the outside (giving us an endoskeleton), insects come packed in an armor-like shield, called an exoskeleton. Like our skin, an insect's exoskeleton comes in layers. First there is the living inner layer, and a tough outer layer called the cuticle (not that there's anything cute about it). Next comes a very fine, thin layer called the epicuticle. When the insect sheds its cuticle, the inner layers are digested and reused for making a new cuticle. The undigestible bits are shed in a way that a bug can literally pop out of its skin and expand to a new size.

Molty Musings

You probably aren't aware of your skin shedding, but if you lost your skin as a snake does you would be. The scales you see on a snake form part of the thinner epidermis. Shedding for a snake involves the actual liquidization of dead skin cells (that's right, they turn to goop). This makes the outer skin get soft and dull, even over the snake's eyes. Soon enough, it's time for the snake to rub its skin off, revealing a glossy new layer underneath! Getting rid of the old skin also helps rid the snake of any parasites that might be living on its epidermis. Most snakes living in temperate weather can do this three to four times a year, and rattlesnakes add a new segment to their rattle each time they shed. Don't be fooled by the old myths saying you can count a rattlesnake's age by the number of rattle segments, though, since the end of the rattle usually breaks off through wear and tear.

"Epidermis Pop-Out"

By the Skin of a Lizard

Some lizards will drop their tails when a predator threatens. The muscular spasms of the dropped tail usually keep the lizard's pursuer occupied long enough for the now tail-less reptile to escape. But there are a few species who will give up more than just a tail. When grasped by a predator, some lizards (a few skinks and geckos) will instantly shed their loosened skin to make their getaway, leaving their attackers only a small taste of what they could have eaten.

Skin Pollution

If skin replaces itself by generating new cells, what happens to all of those older skin cells? Do you think they just magically vanish? Think again. Here's a little secret: around 90% of dust is made from human skin. Those dusty desktops, the dust bunnies under your bed, even the little cloud that rises as you plop onto the sofa...they're all there thanks to you!

I KNOW WHAT YOU'RE THINKING: WHAT IS "HAIR" DOING IN A GUIDE TO THE GROSS? WE ALL HAVE IT. WHEN WE WASH IT, IT SMELLS NICE. SHAMPOO COMMERCIALS FEATURE PEOPLE SHAKING IT OUT EVERYWHERE IN THE MOST PLEASING FASHION. EVEN IN THE ANIMAL KINGDOM, WE TEND TO APPRECIATE A CUDDLE WITH A FUZZY KITTEN RATHER THAN WITH A PRICKLY PORCUPINE. BUT THE TIME HAS COME. ON THIS PAGE YOU MUST STARE AT...

The Horrible Truth of HAIR!

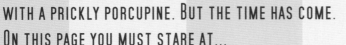

Who Is the Hairiest?

All land mammals have hair, but humans are one of the hairiest. Sound strange? The average human actually has about 5 million hairs on his or her body. Your nose and cheeks are littered with tiny hairs called vellus hairs. All hairs sprout from little pores called hair follicles. We tend to shed around 50 to 100 hairs a day, usually through brushing and shampooing. But don't throw your comb away yet—we also replace most of them. Each hair follicle can grow around 20 new hairs over the course of the human lifespan.

More importantly, all hair is dead! Think about that for a moment. If you lost 100 living hairs a day, and if your barber or hairdresser sliced off living parts of you with a pair of scissors, you'd be screaming in pain. Not to mention gushing blood from your hair. Luckily, this doesn't happen in real life...but I'm glad I made you think about it.

Nit-Pickingly Nasty

Since hair keeps heat close to the body, some creatures take advantage of such a well-insulated abode and call hair "home." For humans, one of the best-known (but not best-loved) hair inhabitants is head lice. These parasitic insects are around the size of a sesame seed and, like vampires, feed on human blood. Head lice have claws that are perfectly adapted for gripping human hair, which makes them hard to remove, and they can multiply quite rapidly—laying up to 100 eggs (known as "nits") during their one-month life cycle.

A Green Sheen!

If you look up in the treetops of Central or South America, you might find a sloth hanging from a branch. Or, rather, you might not. Most sloths are camouflaged to blend into the foliage because of a particular crop they cultivate in the microscopic grooves in their hair. It's in these grooves that single-celled algae thrive—the same slimy green plant that often finds its way into a fish tank.

Priceless Hair?

Would you believe that people used to get excited about digested animal hair? Sometimes a hairball hangs around in the digestive system for so long that the chemical process hardens it into a rock. When goats or other animals hack up these stone-like hairballs, we give them a nice fancy name: a bezoar (bee-zo-ar). It was once believed that bezoars functioned as a remedy against poisons. Queen Elizabeth I of England even kept one with her Crown Jewels. Talk about priceless!

Hack on This

It's not hard to admire the household cat. It's an efficient stalking machine, it smells nice, it poops in its proper place, and its delectable purrs can comfort you to no end. Since a cat spends an awful lot of time licking and grooming itself, it's inevitable that a cat's barbed tongue is going to catch a few hairs with each lick. And hair is by no means digestible. Enter the hairball: your pet pussycat has swallowed too much hair for its own good, and now it is lodged in its intestines. What to do? The cat hacks, coughs, and brings up the slimy ball of undigested hair back out of its system, and onto your floor. Meow Mix it ain't!

A Flood of Blood

On its own, blood is not really a gross thing. Most creatures have some form of it in their systems. Blood circulation is the transport system of the body. It carries oxygen and nutrients to tissues, and it carries waste products away from the tissues. If only every fluid was so helpful. It's when blood gushes out of our bodies that things get gory enough for a gross book. Let's face it: spurting blood is what rates movies Restricted. But not science books!

Bleeding

With a serious slice, a severe slash, or a piercing prick, you can find yourself quickly making a mess of your granny's finest tablecloth. Ever wondered why some cuts bleed more than others? It depends on where and how deeply you cut yourself. If you're unfortunate enough to sever an artery, a vessel carrying blood from the heart to your tissues, you would need emergency medical attention. You may encounter a phenomenon known as "arterial gushing." A watchful eye (and a strong stomach) will spot a gush of blood for every heartbeat.

Who Needs a Head?

Unlike humans, cockroaches do not breathe through nostriles in their heads. They take in air through breathing holes, called spiracles, in their body segments. Oxygen is carried throughout the cockroach's body by internal tubes. Cockroach blood doesn't transport oxygen, which is why their blood doesn't have the rich red hue of oxygenated human blood. And as an insect, a cockroach doesn't have veins and arteries. Its heart pumps fluid, called hemolymph (insect blood), through its body. What would happen if a roach lost its head? There would be no arterial gushing. And the bug could still breathe. A cockroach can live without its head for up to a month if it has had a recent meal. What kills it in the end could be an infection, being eaten, or starvation. It should come as no surprise that roaches have endured for millions of years. Fossils reveal that they were bountiful 300 million years ago, and they're still going strong. Yeah for cockroaches!

Lovely Leeches

There are creatures in this world that will gladly feed on your blood. No, not Count Dracula—leeches! Leeches are dark, cigar-shaped blobs. One leech can suck back up to ten times its body weight in the red stuff. If you look closely, you'll see that the rear end of a leech is a harmless disk-like sucker. The front end bears a nearly hidden sucker with sharp jaws. Chances are, though, a leech bite won't hurt. Leeches secrete a painkiller when they bite as well as an anti-clotting fluid, called hirudin. Hirudin makes blood flow freely, and their job a lot easier.

Scientist A

Did you know that the average adult has around 5 to 6 L (qts.) of blood that circulate through the body over 1,000 times a day?

That's three large pop bottles worth.

"Pop bottle" is not a scientific unit of measurement, Scientist B!

Maybe not, but at least everyone understands me when I talk, Scientist A!

Scientist B

Hideous Healing

From bleeding to healing: when you've cut yourself and the blood begins to flow, the body quickly deals with the problem.

Clotting

Platelets are tiny fragments of cells formed in bone marrow that normally flow freely through the bloodstream. But with a gushing gash, they'll become sticky. Soon, more platelets pile up at the wound, forming a goopy clump that will stop the bleeding. With the help of the platelets, the blood begins to change from a liquid into a gelatinous substance known as a clot. Soon enough, tiny fibers made of protein (called fibrin) form an organic net to bind that cut together.

Scabbing

A scab is really no different than a shield, caking the cut skin with dried-out blood to protect the injury. Underneath, white blood cells are rushing to the scene of the crime, on the hunt for bacteria and other foreign particles that have entered the wound. These white saviors literally digest the bacteria, effectively cleaning out your cut.

A Perfectly Understandable Secretion

Sometimes bacteria and germs get into a cut. And sometimes a wound will start dripping a white creamy fluid, better known as pus. A body produces pus when bacteria that enter the wound from outside are being fended off by the white blood cells. That leaky pus is just the body's way of spitting out the used-up white blood cells, dead bacteria, and bits of dead skin from the wound. Pus may be putrid, but it is also a <u>P</u>erfectly <u>U</u>nderstandable <u>S</u>ecretion. Pus is best served thick and creamy. Watery, darker pus indicates a more serious infection.

Mounds of Maggots

The practice of treating wounds with maggots dates back hundreds of years, but was also noticed during the First World War when army doctors saw that patients with maggot-infested wounds often didn't get infections. Maggots of the green blowfly will eat dead tissue, but avoid munching on living tissue. At the size of a grain of rice, these little white wrigglers (sterilized, of course) can be carefully applied to a putrefying wound. Since they don't have teeth, maggots will release a fluid that dissolves the decaying flesh, which they suck back up. They also secrete an antibiotic that helps to get rid of harmful bacteria.

Scar Gazing

When a scab has lifted away, a wound should have brand new tissue waiting underneath. Scientists call it a cicatrix, but to you or me, we're looking at a scar. A scar isn't exactly new skin, but it's close. It's composed of a tough material made from collagen, a connective tissue that cushions the skin. Larger wounds use so much of the collagen fibers that they're visible as those telltale pink lines. Scar tissue is stronger than regular skin, but it lacks the hairs, sweat glands, and blood vessels. Without blood feeding the cells, the scar will lose its color and turn an off-white, standing out for anyone to see.

Great Moments in Scar History: The Fox and the Shark

Australian Rodney Fox was involved in one of the most notorious Great White shark attacks of the 20th century...and lived to tell the tale. The shark's serrated teeth punctured his diaphragm, broke all his ribs, and ripped open a lung. The wound to his chest and abdomen exposed his spleen, and the main artery from his heart. Quick medical aid and 462 stitches kept Rodney held together, and he made a full recovery. A piece of the shark's tooth is still in his wrist. Fox now studies and helps protect the fish that nearly turned him into ground meat.

Mad About
MUCUS

SNOT. BOOGERS. CALL IT WHAT YOU WANT: SCIENTISTS HAVE DUBBED THIS STUFF MUCUS, A TERRIBLY IMPORTANT SECRETION THAT KEEPS THE PARTS OF AN ANIMAL WORKING CLEANLY AND SMOOTHLY. EVERY HEALTHY BODY HAS IT. BUT WHAT EXACTLY DOES MUCUS DO? THE TRUTH ISN'T PRETTY, SO TAKE A DEEP BREATH.

You've just inhaled a nose full of air, but floating around in it are all sorts of dust particles, dirt, smog, germs, and other things your lungs could do without. The mucus that lines the inside of a nose and windpipe acts like a biological broom to trap and sweep away these particles. The mucus is slowly pushed through the passages to the esophagus, where you swallow it along with the rest of your spit and food. Mucus also protects the surface of your eyes from stuff in the air, the walls of your esophagus and stomach from digestive acids, and lubricates your intestines to help push your digested food along.

To Pick or Not to Pick...

Nose-picking is best left to the foolhardy. Your nasal passages are a breeding ground for bacteria. And your fingers pick up all sorts of germs from doorknobs, money, pets, even used copies of this book. Transferring finger to nostril may cut the nasal lining and cause nosebleeds. Nose-pickers may also be prone to pimples in the nasal area from oils on their fingers. You have been warned.

Fantastic Phlegm

Your moistened saliva, tears, and vomit all include mucus in their list of ingredients. Best of all is phlegm, an accumulation of mucus, say, in the lungs. Lung mucus is great for keeping those organs moist and trapping dirt particles. Phlegm levels increase when you have a cold as your body tries to fight the infection.

A Leaky Faucet

An onslaught of bacteria in the form of a common cold requires a tidal wave of snot to flush them out. Just remember that 95% of your mucus is good old water. When you get a cold, your mucus membranes kick into overdrive, turning your nostrils into a faucet. The green tinge to the boogers in your nostrils is caused by compounds in the mucus, known as peroxidases, which actively kill bacteria and fungi. These same compounds show up in a cut on the skin to prevent infections. Other gross things that are green include pond algae and brussels sprouts.

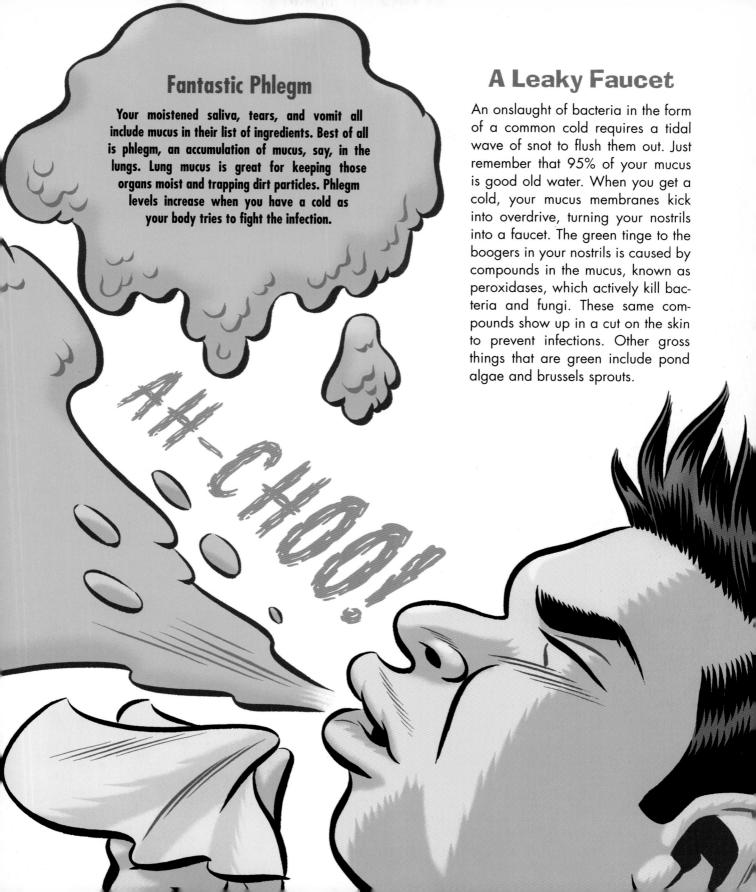

Sweet on Slime

Not Just for Noses!

Not all mucus is found in the nose. Consider our friends the amphibians, like frogs and salamanders. It's fun to try to catch them, but they're hard to keep a firm grip on. Why are they so slippery? Their skin is coated with a layer of mucus, secreted by glands scattered all over their bodies. Amphibians don't just breathe through their lungs, they are also able to absorb oxygen through their thin skin. It helps to keep thin skin moist and slick to prevent drying out. That slippery mucus is also used to dissolve the oxygen passing into amphibians' bodies.

Savory Slug Slime

The banana slug makes the most out of its mucus—it's the secretion with 1,001 uses! A slug is completely drenched in the stuff to help protect it from things like bacteria and pollution, and to help give it a slippery lubricant so it can squeeze itself into tight spaces. Now, let's say a predator like a soldier ant comes along and tries to take a bite out of the slug. The slug will secrete even more mucus, which undergoes a chemical reaction and hardens around the ant's mouth. It's the perfect defensive strategy. The slippery, sticky slug slime also keeps slugs attached to steep inclines and enables them to climb walls. And when it comes time to mate, slugs can follow the trails of slime to find their match! Slug slime is so important that major universities allow their researchers to spend hours studying the stuff. Some scientists have discovered that this sluggy snot can quickly absorb water, causing the slime to swell up to 100 times its original volume.

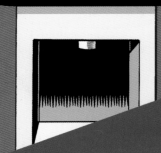

Mucin Mansions

Let's single out a species worth examining for what is perhaps the most creative use of its mucus. In the desert regions of Australia live water-holding frogs, which spend much of their time buried underground (so the sun can't bake them to a crisp). They only emerge during the rainy season to feast on all the bugs they can. But when the rainy season comes to an end and the water begins to dry up, the water-holding frogs suck up all the water they can into huge bladders in their bodies. Then the frogs burrow back underground and cover themselves in a protective layer of their own mucus and skin cells, creating a cocoon that keeps all of that stored water from evaporating away. They can survive for up to two years like this, but usually the frogs just wait until they sense the pitter-patter of rain on the ground above, then rip open their snotty shields to return to the surface to breed.

Mucus on the Offensive

Mucus is a great tool for catching a meal or two. Take, for instance, the larvae of the New Zealand fungus gnat. They live in caves and have the ability to glow in the dark. They also manufacture threads of sticky snot that they lower beneath them like fishing lines. Passing insects are attracted to the light produced by the larvae, but get trapped in the gloopy threads hanging nearby. The gnat larvae then reel in their catches for dinner—snot and all!

The Bolas spider is a master of whipping its sticky webs out to capture moths. It can even produce a chemical that attracts the moth. Maybe that's not playing fair, but who cares—snotty, sticky strands of webs make this page fun!

Saved by Slime

Lurking at the bottom of colder ocean waters is a slender, eel-like scavenger called the hagfish. Most hagfish live in burrows and move about in the soft sediment of the ocean floor. In coastal waters up to around 800 m (over 2,000 ft.) deep, hagfish are responsible for eating most of the sunken carcasses of whales and other large fish on the ocean bottom. If a predator threatens, the hagfish secretes a slime from around 200 glands covering its body. That slime quickly absorbs the surrounding seawater, causing it to expand into a big and blobby mass over 100 times its original volume! The long trail of slime not only deters would-be hunters, but may also suffocate them as well. A hagfish's slime might also be useful to coat its food to keep any other scavengers from taking a nibble. Hagfish slime: truly a multi-purpose goop!

House of Wax
(and Other Leaky, Oozy Things)

If you thought we were finished discussing all sorts of oozy, leaky things...think again! The animal kingdom is positively dripping with things that ooze and leak, and you need to look no further than your own ears to get the scoop on gloop.

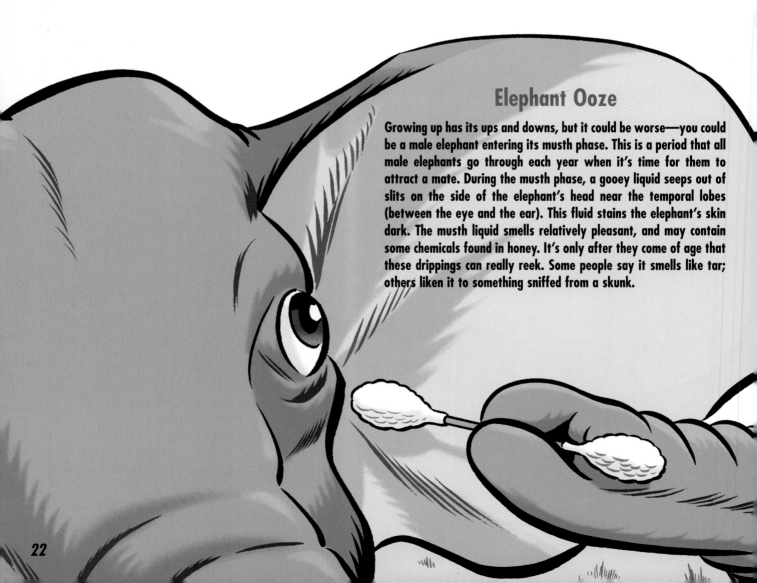

Elephant Ooze

Growing up has its ups and downs, but it could be worse—you could be a male elephant entering its musth phase. This is a period that all male elephants go through each year when it's time for them to attract a mate. During the musth phase, a gooey liquid seeps out of slits on the side of the elephant's head near the temporal lobes (between the eye and the ear). This fluid stains the elephant's skin dark. The musth liquid smells relatively pleasant, and may contain some chemicals found in honey. It's only after they come of age that these drippings can really reek. Some people say it smells like tar; others liken it to something sniffed from a skunk.

An Awful Earful

The skin of your ear canal has over 2,000 glands that leak out a steady stream of cerumen, or as you can call it, earwax. It looks nasty...but it sure is good for you. That cerumen is doing its duty, slowly pushing out all the dirt, dust, grime, and other impurities that get swept inside your ears each day. As the runny wax makes its way to the outer portion of the ear, the outside air dries it off. Clumps of parched wax break up and tumble back outside. This can happen at any time: maybe a choice chunk of wax might even unexpectedly fall into your soup at the dinner table.

If you're a bird called a red-billed oxpecker, then waxy chunks at the dinner table could mean good eating! In one study, oxpeckers could be seen entering the ears of some mammals. Those whose ears were left alone by oxpeckers ended up clogged with earwax. The animals whose ears were pecked at by the oxpeckers were wax-free. Could these birds be nibbling away at the ear candy of others?

The Most Wax in Anyone's Head

Sperm whales can be quite timid, although the males certainly look fearsome with their big, blocky heads. In those heads is a large organ called the case. Inside the case is a waxy oil called spermaceti. Since whales communicate through a series of clicks, some researchers believe that the waxy spermaceti amplifies or even transmits the clicks, but this is only one theory. In the past, whalers hunted the sperm whales for the wax, which is a very useful oil. It was used for signal lamps on American railroads until the end of the First World War.

GAMES YOU SHOULD NEVER PLAY

DINNER IS SERVED! →

"Human Birdfeeder"

Grand Champion of Leaky, Oozy Things

Oozing across the ground as it absorbs decaying matter, a slime mold is like a monster out of an old horror movie. It's an organism that moves around like a single-celled animal...and that's because one kind of slime mold is just that—an enormous single cell. Other slime molds have many cells. Either way, slime molds always ooze their way across the cool, moist earth where they absorb dead matter from their surroundings. But when conditions around it aren't too friendly, this organism takes its cue from a fungus (like mushrooms). The slime mold stops spreading across the ground and grows tall stalks that form clusters of spores. When the spores explode, they send off little cells of slime molds to start their oozing lifestyle all over again.

Pool of Tears

Your pet goldfish Annabelle has just kicked the bucket. You wandered into the kitchen while your mom was chopping onions. The tears have not only welled up in your eyes, but they're streaming down your cheeks, and splashing into puddles on the floor. They're salty, they're snotty, and gross enough to warrant a spot in this book!

Tearing Up

Tears are produced by the lacrimal glands. You have two of these glands located behind the upper eyelid on each of your eyes. The tears flow along tubes called tear ducts, and are then washed across your eyeball with each blink. Tears flow through four drainage tear ducts (two for each eye) between gaps in the eyelids near the nose, which is why crying a lot will make your nose runny.

Scientist A

The human eye produces about a quarter of a teaspoon of tears a day.

Bloodshot!

Crying isn't always the best way to solve a problem. Sometimes tears are not enough. One animal that knows this is the horned lizard. Say a coyote comes sniffing around looking for a quick meal. While some lizards can drop a twitching tail to confuse or frighten their foes, the horned lizard has a unique and gory surprise—it'll build up the blood pressure in its sinuses. When the pressure becomes too great, the sinus wall bursts, and the lizard can shoot a stream of blood from the corner of its eye at its oppressor—up to the length of a picnic table!

Not-So-Lonely Teardrops

There's a lot of water in a tear, but there's a lot of other stuff you probably didn't even know was there.

Lipid Layer – A layer of oils, or lipids—secreted through pores along your eyelids—forms the top layer of a tear. Oil does not evaporate easily, so this layer protects the watery content of your tear from drying out, and leaving your eyes to dry like raisins!

Aqueous Layer – It's here that most of the water in your tear can be found, but it's not just water. Floating around in this solution are proteins, salt, and glucose, giving tears their distinctive taste. And last, but not least, there's the waste product, urea, also found in your urine.

Mucin Layer – The mucin layer may take up less than 0.5% of your tear, but it still has a job to do. That sticky slop makes the rest of the tear stick nicely to the surface of your eye, rather than constantly streaming down your cheeks.

Eye Didn't Want to Know

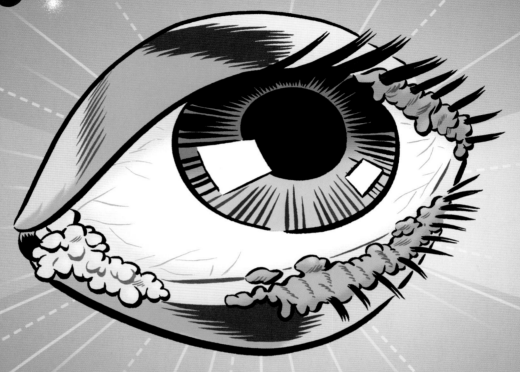

Nameless Gunk

In the morning, when you wake up and walk to the bathroom mirror, you'll probably find little crusted deposits at the corners of your eyes. Believe it or not, there's no actual name for the crusty stuff, but that doesn't mean we're not going to talk about it!

Why is it even there? During the day, you constantly blink, and your eyelashes act as windshield wipers to remove dirt and excess tears. But when you're sleeping, your eyelids remain closed, accumulating a night's worth of sweat, oils, and more tears. This mixture collects in the corner of your eye (known as the caruncle). The air around you evaporates the excess water, and presto! You awake to find the corners of your eyes are all crusted over with the dried-out residual solids.

Bloodshot II: The Sequel

When the West Indian wood snake meets up with a predator, it plays one of the most convincing games of "dead" around. Not only does it lie still, but its eyes turn red as they fill with blood. The blood then seeps out of the snake's mouth, making it look like a fresh corpse (and possibly not quite so appetizing any more).

Watch What You Eat, Unless...!

Frogs and toads can sure keep an eye on their food...literally. Their eye sockets are not enclosed with bone, as ours are. When a frog or toad snatches a meal, their eyeballs go to work, helping to push the food into their stomach.

But enough about the eating habits of frogs, let's talk about their bums! In particular, let's talk about the bum of the South American false-eyed frog. When a predator comes strolling by, the frog does the unthinkable, and moons its attacker! On its bum are two big spots that look like a pair of giant eyes that usually scare the predator away. If that's not enough, the spots can ooze out a foul-smelling liquid that usually is enough to make the predator turn tail.

Scientist A

Yowzers, Scientist B! This is even better than Dandruff Landing Pad!

It's an empty space. They could have at least put a picture there.

Scientist B

Open Up and Say...

Your Mouth: Home to Millions!

You can find it on the scum of a pond. You can find it covering your teeth. We're talking about biofilm, a community of bacteria that has surrounded itself in a protective layer of slime. You might recognize biofilm as the slippery substance on some rocks near a stream, or perhaps on a wet log in a rainy forest. This collection of bacteria occurs in every corner of the globe. A mouth is a great place for biofilm to grow, because it's a warm, wet world teeming with bacteria.

Rotting Teeth

When you gobble sugary sweets, certain sugar-loving bacteria, called *Streptococcus mutans*, move in and break down the leftover sugars coating your teeth. These bacteria excrete a form of acid that eats away at the hard enamel of your teeth, and kills some of the bacteria needed for a healthy mouth. Now you've got problems. Your teeth are rotting, and soon enough, you've got cavities! The bacteria work their way deeper until they reach the center of your tooth called the pulp. It's here that bundles of nerves receive the same acid bath. The result? A pounding toothache, and a visit to the dentist.

R. Ottenteeth

Enter the Dentist

Dentists don't whip out sharp metal instruments simply to scare you. Those pointed picks are needed to scratch off tartar, a gritty substance composed of particles of old food and "layer upon layer" of bacteria that have come to feast upon it. You help get rid of it every time you floss and brush your teeth, but even brushing and scraping can't get rid of all the bacteria.

Unlike beavers, sloths are part of a group of mammals that don't have front teeth. These mammals are called Edentata.

Wow, I guess that means my great-grandfather is an edentate!

Scientist A

Scientist B

A Beaver's Cleavers

Ah, the noble beaver...proud symbol of Canada and one of the world's largest rodents, with some of the craziest teeth you've ever seen. As with all rodents, a beaver's four incisor teeth (two on top and two on the bottom) continue to grow throughout the beaver's life. These incisors are important to a beaver. Beavers have lip flaps that close around their molars, but leave their incisors out in the open. These flaps allow the beaver to swim underwater and carry branches at the same time without getting a mouthful of water. Now, you and I are used to white teeth, but beavers' teeth are covered with an orangey brown enamel, due to the iron in the animals' diet. And just so you know, with their huge chompers, beavers can cut through a piece of wood as thick as a rolling pin in under a minute.

I'm innocent!

29

...Eugh!

Sponging Up Supper

One of the oddest-looking mouths in nature belongs to the house fly. As seen under a microscope, a fly's mouth has sponges instead of teeth. A house fly has a proboscis (the long portion of the mouth), which has a pair of pads used for soaking up liquids. Oh yes, there is liquid involved here...fly spit! That is why you'll find house flies hanging around foods like spilled sugar on your kitchen counter. A fly will dribble saliva onto the sugar, wait until it dissolves, and then slurp it back up through its hollow proboscis. And all it leaves behind is a small stain. How courteous and considerate!

Hooray for Halitosis

Bacteria are responsible for halitosis, a challenging word that means "bad breath." Microbes breaking down the bits of food stuck around your teeth release nasty gases that waft out of your mouth. The stinky gases are produced by bacteria that cannot live in oxygen, so they tend to hang out below the tongue and in between your teeth. They break down bits of food stuck there. Two of the gases they make are hydrogen sulfide (the same smell as rotten eggs), and a volatile sulfur compound (similar to the smell you get in onions and garlic).

Hal I. Tosis

The Deadliest Breath in the World?

We're told that dragons breathe fire, right? We're also told that dragons don't exist. But some of you may know of the Komodo dragon from the island of Komodo (in Indonesia). Measuring up to the size of a ping-pong table in length, it's the world's largest lizard, and the deadliest. Though the Komodo dragon doesn't kill with a blast of fire, its breath has a truly nasty reek. If we were to pry open the dragon's mouth, we'd find large, serrated (jagged) teeth. Since the dragon has no way of flossing, bits of animal carcass remain wedged between the lizard's teeth. Bacteria thrive here. In fact, scientists have found over 50 strains of bacteria in a Komodo dragon's saliva! All of this works to the dragon's advantage. If the Komodo dragon can't kill an animal on the spot, the septic bacteria in its saliva works like a poison, and the victim usually dies from the bite a few days later.

Saved by Saliva!

Luckily, you're producing your own personal mouthwash right now...YOUR OWN SPIT! Saliva contains enzymes that help maintain a healthy community of bacteria in the mouth. Not only that, but saliva is loaded with oxygen molecules—and that's what helps control the populations of bacteria in your mouth. When only a little saliva is flowing, you tend to get stinkier breath. This is what happens in the morning when there's less saliva in one's mouth, causing what is referred to as "morning breath." But when your spit is flowing like water from a faucet, you're more likely to have a satisfying scent coming from behind those lips. People who don't make a lot of spit usually end up with more cavities than those who do.

GAMES YOU SHOULD NEVER PLAY

KISSES 5¢

"Komodo Kissing Booth"

My name is Mortimer

Facts That Will Make You Lose Your Lunch

Sometimes when you're at the dinner table, Mom and Dad might narrow their eyes at you and tell you that you're eating like an animal. If they do, now's your chance to tell them how some animals actually do eat!

Shared Food Is Good Food

The honeypot ant gets the "Weirdest Eating Habit" prize. In a honeypot ant nest some of the workers climb to the ceiling to perform a very important job. Fellow worker ants, returning from gathering nectar, stop to regurgitate some of their stash into the mouths of the ants on the ceiling. The hanging ants' abdomens become so full that they swell to the size of peas. When food for the colony becomes scarce, the bloated ants regurgitate the stored nectar for the rest of the gang to eat.

Voracious Vultures

Unlike most birds, vultures have an acute sense of smell—all the better for catching whiffs of the carcasses they feed on. When they sniff a dead animal, vultures will swoop in for a feast. Using their hooked beaks, vultures tear open their meal (usually through incisions at the eye sockets or near the anus) and poke their heads into the guts to chow down. A vulture's stomach acid is so strong that it will destroy bacteria that cause illnesses. Vultures may be doing you a world of good since they get rid of the bacteria-infested roadkill. It's something to consider before you pass judgment on these flesh-eaters.

Freshly Brewed...With Just a Hint of Feces

Here's a fact you can spring on Mom and Dad while they're having their morning cup of coffee. On some Indonesian islands lives a small marsupial called the palm civet that forages among the trees for ripe red coffee cherries. But the palm civet's stomach can't digest the pits, which pass through its digestive system, landing in little poopy plops on the ground. These fecal gems are collected and processed to make coffee. Enzymes in the animals' stomachs ferment the beans in such a way that the coffee brewed from the excreted beans tastes great. The resulting drink, known as Kopi Luwak, is one of the priciest specialty coffees around.

Good Eats

Ever heard of a vampire that could suck blood for four hours straight? It happens, and the culprit is the flea. Four hours of bloodsucking is more than its stomach can hold. So out comes the blood through the flea's bum, splashing down little drops below it. You might think this wasteful, but think again. The dried-up splashes provide a nourishing meal for the flea's young. Now that's good parenting!

Six-Legged and Scrumptious!

Bugs make their way into just about everything, even into the foods we buy at the grocery store. That's why guidelines are established for how many insects and fragments of insects are permitted to be in the foods we buy. What the heck is an "insect fragment," you might find yourself asking? It's a piece of a bug, like an antenna or a wing. Like a needle in a haystack, these can be difficult to find, but once detected, it's not too difficult for a scientist to figure out what species they belong to.

If eating insects worries you, take comfort in the fact that you're actually eating something nutritious. Most insects contain more nutrients, energy, and protein per gram (ounce) than livestock such as pork, beef, and chicken. That said, bugs can be a source of micro-organisms that can make you sick if you eat them—and not just because you don't like the look or taste.

An Egg-Cellently Disgusting Eating Habit

Can you guess what egg-eating snakes feed on? If you guessed eggs, you're correct (but by no means a genius). The way the snake separates an egg's yolk is particularly notable. The snake's mouth can stretch out to surround an egg far larger than the animal's head. No problem! The egg then moves down into the snake's throat where the shell is crushed open. The yolk and embryo in the egg then move on to the stomach. As for the shell, the egg-eating snake vomits that back up. As of yet, the snake has not figured out how to fry bacon.

Life, they tell me, is a struggle. Anyone who looks at a baby bunny and thinks how cute it is probably doesn't have the mindset of a hunting predator who sees it as dinner. And like it or not, most species are just that: prey. Around three million of all of the species on Earth are parasites, tiny creatures that thrive at the expense of their prey—other animals.

Dinner for Two

There are creatures out there that will feed off your organs, namely worms. Not your garden-dwelling earthworms, but tapeworms, parasites that like to root around in your bowels, sucking on the walls of your intestines. These stringy suckers can enter your body through uncooked pork, beef, or fish. Lacking digestive systems, tapeworms will absorb nutrients from your intestines directly into their own bodies. Tapeworms have knobby heads with hooks so they can clip on to the walls of intestines, and a neck that produces a "tail" of body segments, called proglottids, containing thousands of tapeworm eggs. Their tails can grow to over 4 m (13 ft.) long, and the segments can break off and end up in your poop. So the baby tapeworms are all ready for an exciting life of entering into a pig, cow, or fish (through untreated water), and then to a human, and then to the toilet. what a lovely life cycle!

Chigger Diggers

Chiggers are a branch of the mite family whose young are parasites to most animals. They can be found in grassy, weedy areas, where they lie in wait of passing hosts...even us humans. Chiggers are responsible for chigger dermatitis, a skin rash about as nasty as it sounds. It appears as red spots that are very, very itchy. Chiggers tunnel through your skin by releasing a juice that digests the cells, creating little passageways that are seen as red welts. It's always advisable to wear long pants when going through bushes.

Bugs Drive Bats Batty

Some species of bats gather together in huge numbers. Doing so can keep up their body temperatures during cold spells, but it also gives parasites a huge number of hosts to live on. It's been estimated that around 700 species of mites, insects, and ticks can be found living on the bodies of bats, and there are a few species that are found nowhere else in the world.

This Will Tick You Off

Ticks are bloodsuckers, and they'll feed on whatever they can sink their mouth parts into. The most notorious tick in North America is the deer tick, which is responsible for spreading Lyme disease. After feeding on the blood of mice, these ticks climb onto long spades of grass and wait for deer to come along, to be their next hosts. However, a human will do just as well if one happens to pass by. When it bites, a tick may pass on a bacteria that causes a rash, and makes joints hurt and people sleepy.

[Another Parasitic Page]

How to Bottle a Botfly

It's high time we mention the botfly, of which there are various species. One likes to lay its eggs in the nostrils of toads. When the eggs hatch, the maggots proceed to eat the toad's skull out. There's also a species that likes human hosts, but the fly—perhaps aware that humans can wield fly swatters—is clever enough not to land on us. Instead, the botfly lays her eggs on the underside of a mosquito. The mosquito then finds a human to suck blood from, and the body heat causes the eggs to hatch. The botfly larvae burrow into the skin. So how do you get these maggots out of your skin? The best way is to get a slab of meat and place it over the wound, which lures the little wrigglers to the surface. The maggots will dig into the meat, leaving you maggot-free.

Making a Meal of Mommy

Birth can be a real killer...especially for the parent. That's what happens in some cases of parthenogenesis, a big word that means being able to give birth without mating. This occasionally happens to insects called gall midges. Unfortunately, the young grow inside the flesh of their mother. When it comes time for the larvae to mature, they eat their way out of their mom and fly off to begin the cycle all over again.

Nauseating Nursery

It's not easy raising kids, especially when you hatch more than 100 of them at a time. When it comes to finding food, some animals can't afford to play nice. Braconid wasps are a diverse family of parasitic wasps with a particularly ruthless—and deadly—means of raising their young. Before the female wasp lays her eggs, she searches for fresh food—so fresh that it's still alive. A juicy caterpillar usually does the trick. One species of female Braconid wasp has a sharp, needle-like organ on her body. It's through this that she injects her eggs into the flesh of the caterpillar. Inside the caterpillar, the eggs grow and develop. When they hatch, the Braconid larvae are surrounded by food—the innards of the caterpillar! They slowly eat the caterpillar from the inside out, leaving behind an empty, hollowed-out husk.

Uuuurp!

GAMES YOU SHOULD **NEVER PLAY**

"Braconid Inside-Out Bread"

What a Gas!

WHERE WOULD WE BE WITHOUT GAS? NOT THE LIQUID THAT MAKES OUR CARS RUN BUT THE AIRY SUBSTANCE THAT FORMS PLANETS LIKE SATURN, THE EARTH'S ATMOSPHERE, AND EVERY ANIMAL FART AND BURP ON THE PLANET.

Blame it on the Air

The main component in a burp is gas from the outside air that gets swallowed in your stomach. There's nothing for your stomach to do with this air, except return it from where it came. So back it goes, all the way up your throat and out your mouth in a big, beefy burp. That nasty belchy smell comes from the digesting food and stomach acid the burp brings up as it travels back up your throat and into the great, wide world again.

Scientist A

A normal person may pass gas around fourteen times a day.

Anatomy of a Fart

A good, hearty fart is an entirely different kind of gas. Farts form deep inside the coils of your bowels, where waste products of digestion are formed, like methane gas, carbon dioxide, and hydrogen. These are made by bacteria that live in your guts. There's also some oxygen and nitrogen in a fart, which comes from the air swallowed along with the rest of whatever is skewered at the end of your fork. None of these gases smells. It's the trace amounts of sulfur gases hissing out our bums that will wrinkle noses. The more sulfur in your food, the more foul the flatulence. Meat is the prime culprit for a stinky one. Beans are also notorious for causing gas attacks, but the gas produced is the result of indigestible sugars they contain.

Naughty Noises

The trademark sound of a fart is caused by gas whipping through a tensed sphincter, the muscular valve controlling the opening to your anus. Like air escaping from a balloon, sonic farts depend on the speed of the escaping gas and how tightly your sphincter is closed.

S.B.D.'s (Silent-But-Deadlys) are known for slowly seeping out into the air, catching nearby neighbors off guard. A little-known, or smelled, fart is the S.D. (Silent-Deathly), escaping from the anus of a freshly deceased animal body. Gases in a fresh corpse usually find their way out, but by that point the farter isn't too concerned about offending anyone.

Scientist B

That's too bad, because the human nose can detect over 10,000 different odors.

Gassing Up

Mondo Methane

Methane-makers come in all shapes, and can be big or small. Ruminants, like sheep and cows, have complex stomachs containing bacteria that break down the grasses these animals munch on. They're the major animal methane-makers on the planet. In fact, the farting and belching of one sheep in a day could power a small truck for around 40 km (25 mi.)! Tiny little termites also feast on plant matter, and like the ruminants, little micro-organisms in their guts break down the plant matter and give off methane gas. Though one termite's fart is hardly noticeable, if you were to gather all of the termites in the world and let them fart in unison, you'd be engulfed in a huge cloud of methane gas. The yearly estimate for the world's termite methane production is around 20 million tonnes.

Scientist A

A sheep makes around 30 L (8 gal.) of methane gas a day.

That's 15 pop bottles!

A cow can produce up to 200 L (53 gal.) of methane, though.

That's 100 bottles of pop on the wall, 100 bottles of pop. Take one down, pass it around...

99 bottles of pop on the wall.

Scientist B

Breathing through Your Bum

Young dragonflies have fantastic rear ends. They're muscular and big and contain rows of plate-like gills. Not only do their bums look amazing, but they serve one of the most important functions of all—dragonflies breathe through them. The big muscles pump in the water, and the gills take in oxygen from the water. Then the dragonflies swish out the old water through their anuses and repeat the process.

Boiling Bums!

Talk about deadly gases! When attacked, bombardier beetles shoot boiling farts at their enemies in rapid succession. The foul spray is a mixture of chemicals that the beetles keep stored away in two internal pouches close to their rear ends. When the beetles are bugged, they mix these two liquids, causing a chemical reaction that releases so much heat that the resulting cocktail actually boils into a gas.

Portrait of the Artist as a "Fartist"

Bombardier beetles aren't the only creatures with a gift for flatulence. As a child, Joseph Pujol (1857–1945) discovered he had a very special talent: by contracting his abdominal muscles, he could suck water up his rectum and squirt it out with the force of a garden hose. Later dubbed "Le Pétomane" (which, translated into English, means "Fartist"), Pujol toured France, hung out with famous artists like Renoir and Matisse, and for three years performed at France's fanciest venue, the Moulin Rouge. He could blow out candles with his bum from a table length away and control his sphincter to "sing" famous songs. Talent clearly lies within.

Things That Go "Boom!"

Explosions are everywhere in the universe. They happen on the sun, and people say it's because of the "Big Bang" that we're here in the first place. It's when explosions happen on the organic level that we turn our heads, plug our noses, and get grossed out.

Put the "Fun" Back in Fungi

It's not a plant! It's not an animal! It's a fungus—an organism that decomposes other organisms to absorb their nutrients. There are many types of fungi, including toadstools, molds and athlete's foot, a fungus that grows on living creatures like you and me. The fungi familiar to most people is a mushroom with its dome-like cap and deep-rooting stem. When it comes time for the fungus to multiply, that mushroom cap literally explodes, sending spores (fungus "seeds") into the air to begin the cycle again.

Hopping, Popping Toads

In the Amazon lives the Surinam toad, which probably cares more about the bumps on its skin than your average teenager. When it comes time to mate, the father of the toads-to-be moves 60 to 80 of his wife's fertilized eggs onto her back. Then the skin on her back swells up and surrounds the eggs. Over the next few months, the eggs develop until finally the young are ready to hatch. Like something out of a monster movie, these little toads break free by digging through the skin on their mother's back.

Exploding Airbags!

Most fish keep themselves afloat with the help of a swim bladder, a gas-filled bag stored in their bodies. A fish can adjust the size of the bladder to help keep it at a constant depth. If that fish is suddenly snatched from deep water at the end of a fishing line, it may not be able to change the amount of gas in its bladder fast enough to adapt to the rapidly changing water pressure. As the fish is brought to the surface, the water pressure around it decreases, and the gas in the swim bladder expands until the fish's organs and tissues rupture and the gas is released.

Ejectable Organs

The sea cucumber, a bottom-dwelling invertebrate, looks like a green-brown version of the salad vegetable. When an enemy comes to take a bite out of a sea cucumber, this animal gives them more than a mouthful. Some species will literally turn themselves inside-out, spewing their guts at the attacker, allowing the cucumbers to make a not-so-clean getaway.

Your Very Own Ticking Time Bomb

If we were to unzip your skin and take a look inside, we'd find a small tube-like appendage positioned where the large and small intestines meet. It's called the appendix. It doesn't really serve any major purpose, although it can prove to be a life-threatening nuisance. The appendix can get blocked by digested food traveling through the small intestine and become inflamed. If it isn't treated, it may unexpectedly rupture due to a build-up of mucus and lack of blood circulation. A burst appendix can be life-threatening, and requires an operation.

An Ant Not to Be Ant-Agonized

Nature is full of exploding things, but there are few creatures, like a certain ant species in Malaysia, that make the ultimate sacrifice and go BOOM! These ant soldiers are packed with some serious internal TNT. A toxic chemical is produced in two big glands that run from their mandibles, or jaws, to their bums. When an enemy threatens, the soldiers contract their muscles so hard that their abdomens explode. The enemy is lethally assaulted with a gory SPLAT of the soldiers' sticky, chemical-covered guts.

Spectacular Stenches

LOTS OF THINGS CAN MAKE A STINK — OURSELVES INCLUDED! HERE ARE A FEW THINGS THAT MAY MAKE YOUR STOMACH TURN.

A Skunktacular Stench

Skunk spray originates at the skunk's rear end, in two glands about the size of large grapes, where a chemical solution is stored. Even skunks don't like to get hit with a jet of their own spray, and will only use the stuff sparingly. If a predator comes by, the skunk tries to intimidate: raising its tail threateningly, clicking its teeth, and hissing. If the skunk's little show fails to ward off enemies, the skunk can spray its musk up to 5 m (16 ft.). The skunk can control that stinky juice like you or I would a garden hose—from a powerful jet of water to a cloud of misty spray.

Putrid Plants

We like to think nice thoughts about plants and flowers. They produce fresh oxygen, and their blooms tend to give off lovely aromas that make us all smile. Well, think again! There are some plants that stink. One of the main culprits is an Asian fruit called the durian. At first glance, you wouldn't think much of eating it. It's a football-sized orb covered in spikes. Crack one of those open and you get a fleshy fruit that many people in that part of the world crave. But along with the tasty fruit, you get a sickening smell that has been likened to rotting food or garbage. In fact, in Singapore, "no durian" signs have been placed in some public areas.

Pondering Perfume

Perfume is by no means a recent invention. Through the ages, humans have tried to stifle our own body odor—sometimes by covering it up with scents that come from animals. We're not talking about eau d'elephant, or bottled yak spit—these are highly prized perfumes!

A musk scent comes from a species of deer that lives in Asia and Eastern Russia. More specifically, it comes from a sac near the front of the deer's abdomen. Fluid in this sac gives off a distinctive aroma, and is mainly used to help the deer attract females during the mating season. For any humans wanting musk of their own, hunters have to kill the deer, cut off the sac, and dry it out. Around 10 kg (22 lbs.) of musk are used in perfumes each year. Since it's been estimated that you need to kill around 160 musk deer in order to get 1 kg (2 lbs.), you can see why the animal is protected.

Another animal that is hunted for its scent is the sperm whale. Around 1 in 100 sperm whales produce a dark, waxy secretion in their intestines called ambergris. In its raw state, ambergris smells pungent, but as it ages, its smell gets a bit better. Ambergris is very good at preserving smells, and was a big ingredient in early perfumes for this quality. It was once the most valuable of all whale products. Today we have banned the practice of killing sperm whales for their smelly guts, although if you're lucky enough, you might find a chunk or two lapping up against your feet on the shore. Just maybe.

45

[And Other Sweet Smells]

SWEAT: WE ALL DO IT, AND WE'LL USUALLY DO EVERYTHING IN OUR POWERS TO CONCEAL IT. BUT NOW IT'S TIME TO TAKE A STAND AND REVEAL IT. WITH A GRAND TOTAL OF TWO TO THREE MILLION SWEAT GLANDS EACH, WE OUTSWEAT ANY ANIMAL ON THE FACE OF THE PLANET.

Don't Sweat It, Sapien!

We *Homo sapiens* have two different kinds of sweat glands. The eccrine glands, found all over the body, produce an acidic, watery fluid, which is secreted all over our skin. This happens all the time, twenty-four hours a day, seven days a week.

The sweat from your apocrine glands is quite a different story. As fetuses in our mothers' wombs, we have these all over our bodies, but after we're born they're only found in places like our armpits, navels, ears, and down in our privates. Apocrine sweat doesn't become fully functional until puberty hits. Then you'll start to secrete a thick, waxy gray substance diluted by fluid from other nearby glands. Stress and emotion are factors in how much of this oozes out on to you. So any older siblings and parents worried that you're learning a bit too much might be making some scented sweat of their own...right now.

Skin of Salt

Sweat gets water from down in the bloodstream, mixing it with salt and other essential ingredients. The sweat is passed to the surface of the skin through your pores. The salt is usually reabsorbed back into the bloodstream, but in a heavy sweat, excess salt slips onto the surface of the skin. That's why your pet pooch likes to lick you—not so much out of love, but because you've become a human salt-lick.

BROMOHYDROSIS

HYPERHYDROSIS

Challenge of the Big Words!

Each of these long words has something to do with sweat. Learn what they mean, then impress your friends with *Gross Universe's* patented "scientific know-how." Answers on page 63.

Arduous Odors

With all that glistening sweat, you're probably thinking that a wetter person is a smellier person. But you'd be absolutely wrong! Sweat doesn't make you reek; it's the bacteria that feed off your sweat that do. Bacteria absolutely love warm, wet crevices where they can breed. Sweaty armpits and navels are perfect for these breeding bacteria. Here, they feed on your fluids, and their waste begins to stink up your body. Showering and bathing will never get rid of all of the microbes living on your skin, but it helps to keep their numbers down and keep you stinking less.

Eccrine Sweat Ingredients:

Water
Sodium Chloride (salt)
Potassium Salts
Urea
(the solid ingredient in human pee)
Lactic Acid
(waste product from metabolism)

Smelling Success

Imagine you are at a birthday party and you meet somebody new. What is your first reaction? A handshake? A "hello"? Sniffing this new person's butt? Butt-sniffing is a common thing...just not among humans. Dogs recognize each other mainly by scent. Sniffing another dog's butt reveals a great deal of information: what sex the other dog is, if it's ready for mating, its status among other dogs, and what it last ate. If dogs in the same area have a similar status, they will smell each other's bums at the same time. But a higher-ranking dog gets the first sniff!

You're in the Urine

OF ALL OF THE FLUIDS PRODUCED BY ANIMALS, URINE IS JUST ABOUT THE MOST USEFUL. IT'S NOT ONLY A WASTE PRODUCT, BUT IT'S ALSO GREAT FOR CLEANING WOUNDS, MARKING TERRITORY, OR ATTRACTING A MATE.

Waste Not, Want Not

Pee is the body's liquid waste. Every time you pee, you're getting rid of a solution that is roughly 95% water and 5% dissolved solids. Those solids include sodium chloride (salt), and a chemical compound known as urea.

Urea is a safer form of a toxic waste product called ammonia, which the liver transforms into urea before adding a shot of water to make pee. It's that strong ammonia smell that can give urine its sharp scent.

Scientist A

In case you were wondering, the average human adult pees out around 1.5 L (qts.) of urine a day.

That's three-quarters of a pop bottle full of pee.

In a week, that makes 10.5 L (qts.).

That's just over 5 pop bottles full.

In a month, that is about 45 L (qts.).

That's roughly 22 pop bottles full.

In a year, that makes 547.5 L (qts.).

That's roughly 274 pop bottles full.

In one lifetime, Scientist B, it's approximated that you'll produce around 36,000 L (qts.) of urine!

Well, Mr. Smarty Pants, that would equal roughly 18,000 pop bottles full!

Oh yeah? And how many drinking boxes would that make?

Since drinking boxes are around 200 mL (7 oz.) that would make 180,000 drink boxes.

Ugh. I give up with you.

Scientist B

Color Your World

The liver produces a waste product from the breakdown of red blood cells called bilirubin. It contains the pigments that give your urine that sunny yellow shine.

Depending on how much water you have in your system, your kidneys will produce different concentrations of urine. On a hot, sweltering day, when you've perspired a lot and your body has less fluid, you're likely to have darker urine. Your urine will be more highly concentrated than those days when your body is full of fluid and you've got nothing better to do than sit at home and suck back the apple juice.

The Tinkle Teacher

Urine has also been used as an effective teaching tool. As part of his dramatic classroom demonstrations in organic chemistry at Princeton University, professor Hubert Alyea would hand out small crystals for willing students to taste. Anyone up to the challenge would instantly experience the ultimate sour candy, one that turned a tongue ice cold and made it feel as if it were about to shrivel like a raisin. But this wasn't candy, it was concentrated urea, the solid ingredient in urine (just nowhere near enough to do them any actual harm)!

Yum... apple juice!

Health inspectors looking for mice or rats in restaurants don't need mousetraps or cheese to lure any interloping rodents. A quick scan with an ultra-violet (UV) light will detect their urine. Fresh rodent urine glows blue-white, turning yellow as it gets older.

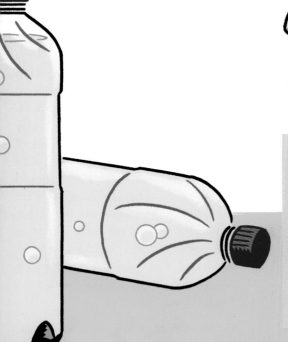

Mind Your Pees and Q's

Useful Urine

Urine is useful? Is it possible? In a word, yes. People have been using their pee for thousands of years, and not just for watering the plants. Fresh urine is sterile—the only germs it contains are the ones it picks up in the urethra on the way out. With this in mind, it should come as no surprise that urine is an excellent way to wash out a wound, providing there's no fresh water in the vicinity. In fact, soldiers used to wash out their wounds on the battlefield by simply taking a tinkle on the infected area.

In the rest of the animal kingdom, urine has been used for a number

Save Your Urine and Save Your Life

How do animals survive in the harsh winter of the far north? Sure, those muskoxen have heavy, hairy coats, but is that enough? Sometimes you've got to do more than just wear a lot of hair...you've got to practice proper urine management.

Larger animals, like the muskox, eat less than a quarter of the amount of food in winter as they do in summer, producing less than a quarter of their summer pee. Arctic grazers reuse urea in their bloodstream by returning it to the rumen, a specialized chamber in the stomach of animals that digest tough grasses through a series of regurgitations. In the rumen, bacteria break down the urea to create a sort of protein that the animals can use to conserve body heat and energy. The extra energy is not used for snowball fights.

Some smaller animals in cold climates concentrate their valuable urea, only letting it out in little spurts to keep from turning into icicles.

of purposes. First, it's a great way to cool off. Take the cute white-faced capuchin monkey, for example. A tree-dweller, it washes its hands and feet with its own urine to help keep cool, and probably communicates social information to other capuchin monkeys within its group with its urine. And let's say you're a hoofed mammal in love. You've got to attract your man. What to do? Letting loose a stream of the yellow stuff actually works wonders. The males can sniff the chemicals in the female urine that communicates her interest to mate. Love is definitely in the air (and bladder).

Flee from Pee

A slender, spaghetti–like parasite, the candiru catfish, can be found in the Amazon River. Scientists speculate that it follows the scent of uric acid in the water, a waste product produced in the gills of other fish. When it picks up a strong signal, the candiru follows the trail then enters the gills of the host fish, using its spiny fins to plant itself firmly inside the flesh. Here, it will gorge itself on its host's blood. If a human enters the river and decides to have a pee in the water, that person could be in for more than he or she bargained for. The candiru, possibly thinking the uric scent is coming from a fish, could swim into whatever uric-acid producing human crevice is available, then use its spiny fins, and...come on, you don't need me to tell you the rest of this, do you?

Scientist A

As a scientist, it is my sworn duty to call a muskox by its proper Latin taxonomic term, *Ovibos moschatus.*

As your sworn nemesis, it is my duty to call a muskox by its Inuit name, *omingmak,* which sounds just as neat and means "animal with skin like a beard."

Scientist B

Origin of the Species' Feces

THINK ABOUT IT: TWENTY-FOUR HOURS A DAY, SEVEN DAYS A WEEK, OUR PLANET IS GETTING BOMBARDED WITH PLOP IN EVERY IMAGINABLE SHAPE AND SIZE.

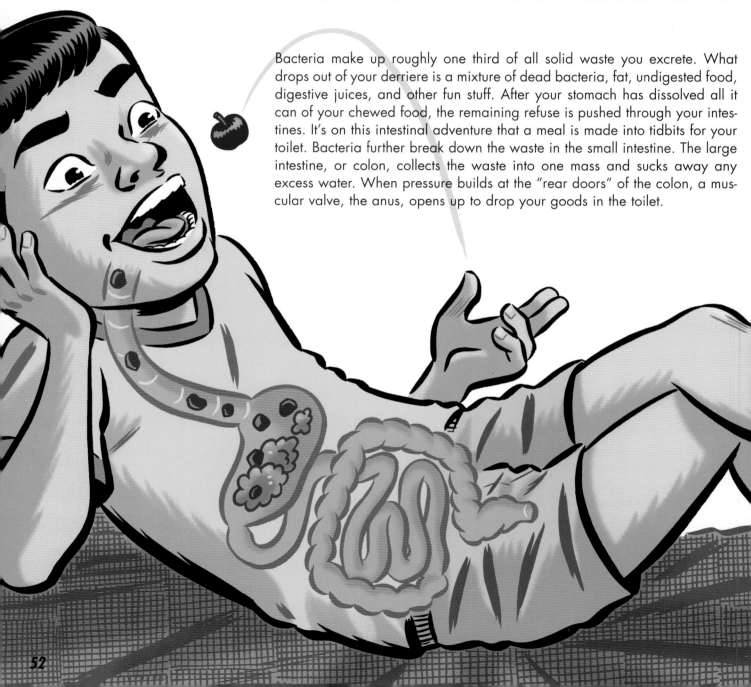

Bacteria make up roughly one third of all solid waste you excrete. What drops out of your derriere is a mixture of dead bacteria, fat, undigested food, digestive juices, and other fun stuff. After your stomach has dissolved all it can of your chewed food, the remaining refuse is pushed through your intestines. It's on this intestinal adventure that a meal is made into tidbits for your toilet. Bacteria further break down the waste in the small intestine. The large intestine, or colon, collects the waste into one mass and sucks away any excess water. When pressure builds at the "rear doors" of the colon, a muscular valve, the anus, opens up to drop your goods in the toilet.

The Ultimate Questions

Universal questions have endured for generations: How big is an infinite universe? Is there life on other planets? And perhaps the most pressing of all, why is poop brown? I am pleased to announce that a component of your bile, a fluid that aids digestion, is a brown-yellow pigment called bilirubin, the remains of decomposing red blood cells. Since bile travels down into your intestines, it's added to the mixture that ends up as feces, and consequently paints it a dirty brown.

And why does poop smell so bad? We've already established that bacteria play a large role in the formation of poop, and also do a good job of breaking down foods. The stench of feces comes from nitrogen compounds produced by bacterial activity.

Scientist A

In the gut, much of the bilirubin is converted into urobilinogen, which then gets converted to stercobilinogen, which is then oxidized by exposure to air in the gut to stercobilin.

Conserving Water?

Not all plops are created equal. A healthy human poop is around three-quarters water. Less than 50% water means you have extreme constipation. When your waste accumulates in the bowels for too long, the colon may absorb more water from your fecal matter than it usually does. With less moisture, your poop begins to dry out like cement, resulting in a parched condition known as constipation. Squeezing out these jagged lumps can be mighty painful. But consider the case of some desert animals that need to conserve as much water as possible. They make hard, dry plops that are almost certain to kick up dust clouds when they land.

Over 90% water content indicates that the intestines are not absorbing enough liquid out of the waste. Then your anus releases a runny syrup that paints the toilet with sickly brown-green squirts. That gloopy poop burning your bum is diarrhea, and there are a few causes for this: a bacterial infection from food poisoning, a stomach virus, or even a stressful day can send you running for the porcelain throne.

Scientist B's Names for Polite Poo:

Feces • Dung • Stool • Scat Droppings • Bowel Movement

The School of Stool

Disguised As Dung

If you're a caterpillar, you're a choice meal for many predators in the animal kingdom. You're soft, you're juicy, and full of nutrients! Caterpillars have had to evolve to keep predators at bay, or else there'd be nothing for them to do but crawl around wearing big "Eat Me" signs. Few are as clever (or gross) as the giant swallowtail caterpillar. It mimics the shape and color of a big globby bird dropping (assuming that birds aren't interested in eating their own doo-doo). And like the ugly duckling that became a swan, this master of disguise eventually turns into a beautiful butterfly.

Fecal Feasting

Human poop retains around 8% of the nutritional value of the food it came from. But while we don't eat our waste, there are many animals who do dine on dung. The animals that win the award for licking their poopy plates clean are termites. They will feast on their own excrement again and again until they've taken as much nourishment out of it that they can. Oh, and when termites have extracted all of the nutrients from their droppings, they use the leftover paste to help build their massive nests. Gives new meaning to the expression waste not, want not.

Finely Fashioned Feces

Let's imagine you're an insect larva. Your job is to eat and grow and eat and grow. Because you're always eating, you are always excreting. Usually, you'll just do your business and move on, but if you're the larva of the tortoise beetle, you've come up with a defensive tactic that puts your poop to good use. You use a part of your bum called an "anal turret," which allows strings of your poop to curve to the left or right. Soon enough, you've covered yourself in a golden-colored thatch of your own excrement. It's quite unappetizing, and deters most predators. Isn't using your imagination fun?

Dive-Bomb Droppings

While feces may be life-sustaining to animals like the termites, it can be lethal to others. Consider the colonies of fieldfare birds living in northern Europe. They may look like ordinary birds, but cross them the wrong way and they become an air force to be reckoned with. When a hunting bird or animal comes near, the fieldfares take to the sky and unleash a wave of droppings onto their opponent. Their attacks are not only disgusting but almost always effective. If the enemy is another bird, the combined splatter will ruin the bird's feathers and possibly even kill it.

V Is for Vomit

BARF. PUKE. TOSSIN' THE COOKIES. CALL IT WHAT YOU WILL, BUT THROWING UP IS NEVER PRETTY. FIRST THERE'S THAT WAVE OF NAUSEA, THEN YOUR MOUTH BEGINS TO SALIVATE, YOUR FOREHEAD GOES CLAMMY WITH SWEAT, YOUR THROAT CLOSES UP, AND BEFORE YOU KNOW IT, YOU'RE RUNNING LIKE AN OLYMPIAN TO THE NEAREST TOILET....

BLECH! Vomit is the forceful throwing up of your stomach contents (known as chyme) by a strong respiratory reflex. When you vomit, your diaphragm (a sheet of muscle in your abdomen that moves your chest when you breathe) squeezes down, your abdominal walls push in, the valve from the stomach to the small intestine closes up, and your stomach muscles rocket the food back up your esophagus. Next thing you know, it's flying out of your mouth like a biological catapult, in whatever direction your mouth is pointing: in the toilet, on the floor, maybe even over the window ledge onto a bed of petunias.

Going through the Motions

Why is it that your stomach can find driving so off-putting? Constant jiggling during travel overstimulates the motion-sensing cells located in your inner ear. But if you're not looking out the window, you can't see why you're getting bumped. Your eyes tell your brain everything's nice and still; and your ears are trying to keep you balanced. Your brain receives so many conflicting messages that some of them "spill over" to activate the vomiting center in the brain. Soon enough, your parents are going to have to scrub the upholstery. So, the next time you spew on a plane, don't blame the catering. Blame your brain.

Honeybee Hurl

Honeybees can't use buckets to gather nectar from flowers. They use a different kind of pail to take nectar back to the hive. A forager bee visits a flower to slurp nectar down into a storage stomach. Returning to the hive, the forager regurgitates the nectar onto the mouth parts of a waiting house bee. House bees swallow and regurgitate the nectar about 50 times, turning the nectar and stomach juices into a thick syrup. After adding a preserving enzyme, the house bee deposits the processed nectar into a honeycomb cell. This bee syrup, known as honey, is best spooned into tea.

GAMES YOU SHOULD NEVER PLAY

"Homemade Honey"

Recipe for
Vomit à la Roast Beef Sandwich

Ingredients

1. Mucus
2. Saliva
3. Acids and chemicals for digestion
4. Bile
5. Roast Beef Sandwich

Directions

1. Chew and swallow sandwich. Allow gastric juices to begin digestion.

2. Come down with an illness (stomach flu, for example) or have a bad reaction to the sandwich. Food poisoning will do just fine.

3. Observe the effects of nausea: sweating, going pale, excess saliva.

4. Run for the toilet.

5. Through a respiratory reflex, bring up chyme.

6. Flush and rinse out mouth.

7. Repeat the above steps as often as desired.

NOTE: The acidity of your stomach can burn the lining of your esophagus, so try not to desire repeating the above steps too often.

H Is for Hurl

ACTUAL LENGTH OF BABY FULMAR PROJECTILE VOMIT

Mommy's Miserable Mornings

Somewhere between one and two months after your mom got pregnant with you, she might have had a lot of nausea and vomiting. This can affect up to 70% of pregnancies, and there are a couple of theories to explain why. One is that the relaxation of the smooth muscle of the stomach wall (which happens during pregnancy) might play a role. Another theory is that hormonal changes in your mom's body tamper with the vomiting center, which results in what your mom calls "morning sickness." While the cause of this is not well understood, the outcome is the same. Yes, you literally made mommy sick.

Things to Call Your Vomit

MEDICAL NAMES
Emesis
Vomitus

NAMES TO TELL THE FOLKS
Throw Up
Vomit

NAMES TO TELL YOUR FRIENDS
Puke
Hurl
Upchuck
Spew
Tossin' the Cookies
Ralph
Barf

Things Not to Call Your Vomit

Sally
Mortimer
Grandma
Your Majesty
Filing Cabinet

REMEMBER: Vomit is not for playing with. That's what basketballs are for.

This One's for the Birds

Young birds aren't able to leave the nest and catch food on their own, so their folks go out to find food for them, but that means leaving the young alone in the nest. How do you protect them? The answer's easy for a fulmar. You let them protect themselves with a defense mechanism of nauseating proportions. At first glance, this young seabird seems pretty defenseless in its rocky seaside nest—the perfect prey for a passing eagle. Think again. As the predator swoops in for a kill, the baby fulmar opens its mouth and lets loose with a jet of vomit! This isn't your everyday all-purpose vomit, but consists of a rich oil the birds make in their stomach for defensive use. There's usually enough in the fulmar's stomach for two to three rounds of this awful assault. Even as new hatchlings, they can projectile vomit up to 30 cm (12 in.) away.

Great skuas are seabirds that will cause other birds to vomit in order to steal their chyme and eat it for lunch.

Scientist B, you just stole my fact—stay away from my lunch!

Scientist B

Scientist A

Foul Fossils AND Putrid Prehistory

NOW THE TIME HAS COME. LET'S WANDER BACK, WAY BACK, IN TIME. WE'RE GOING BACK TO A TIME BEFORE ANY HUMAN WAS AROUND TO WRITE ABOUT GROSS STUFF. BUT EVEN WITHOUT HUMANS ON THE SCENE, THERE WAS PLENTY OF GROSS ACTION.

Dino Dung

Over time, things left in or on the ground can turn into fossils—evidence of ancient life. A coprolite is what polite scientists (who study prehistoric plop) call fossilized feces. Coprolites are pretty useful when we want to explore the eating habits of ancient animals. If you've ever glanced into the toilet and taken a good long look at your doo-doo (come on, admit it), you'll sometimes notice that not everything you eat gets digested (bits of corn and other vegetables come to mind). And that's just what happened to dinosaur poop. As the years convert the feces into fossils, lingering bits of bone, seeds, and plant matter stay encased in their poopy prisons, waiting for the men and women of science to unlock their secrets. Believe it or not, coprolites are also collectors' items, and there are shops where you can purchase prehistoric plop.

LOT 3 Dino Poop

Possibly Prehistoric Pee

Some scientists are getting excited about what could be some of the oldest pee stains ever seen. In the Comanche National Grasslands in Colorado, a bunch of dinosaur footprints have been found. Near the footprints is a 3-m (10-ft.) long, 30-cm (12-in.) deep rut in the earth. It's no footprint. Some scientists are guessing that this little trench might be the result of a dinosaur unloading the contents of its bladder. In an experiment in Georgia, dinosaur urine marks were mimicked by pouring fluid from a big bucket to the ground from a height of 1 m (3 ft.)—presumably that's how high up some dinosaurs' private parts were. All in the name of science!

Very Old Vomit

Recently, scientists have found a hunk of fossilized vomit that dates back 160 million years—the oldest known vomit in the world. It was puked up by an ichthyosaur, a large marine reptile that resembled a dolphin, only not so cute. The ichthyosaur barf contains the remains of belemnites, now-extinct squidlike animals. How do we know that ichthyosaurs puked up their table scraps? Using a scanning electron microscope, scientists were able to locate acid-etching marks that would have been made in the ichthyosaur's guts.

URRRP!

A Beetle's Ball

It's hard to believe that so much of the book has gone by without mentioning the dung beetle. This is an insect that collects bits of other animals' feces, which it rolls along the ground. As the feces is rolled, it turns the dung beetle's booty into a round ball. Once the dung beetle reaches its underground nest, the mother beetle lays her eggs in the dung balls. When the larvae hatch, they find the dung ball just as appetizing as an infant finds a warm bottle.

So what does this have to do with prehistory? If dinosaurs were pooping, then there were other animals that were breaking that poop down—and considering the size of the dinosaur's droppings, there was probably a lot of excrement to decompose. New evidence reveals that during the Late Cretaceous Era (over 65 million years ago), dung beetles were busy storing and feasting on dinosaur doo-doo.

L Is for Leftovers

Congratulations! You've nearly reached the end of the book. If you've stayed up late to read this, you probably want a nice warm bath and then perhaps to crawl under the covers and get some shut-eye. But wait! Before you do, take a look at this last page. I'm sure you'll be left with a few more pressing things to think about.

Cheyletus

These guys live near the dust mites that you met on page six, but they're bigger, they're scarier, and, oh yes, they eat the dust mites. This doesn't give you an excuse not to wash your pillow, because the Cheyletus excrete a liquid that dries into a speck of poop.

Speaking of pillows and mites and anal pellets, consider this: Older pillows weigh more than newer pillows. Why? The reason is that older pillows contain all of the mite poop, dead mites, dead Cheyletus, skin cells, and other revolting bits and pieces that accumulate over the years. Sweet dreams....

Watery Wrinkles

If you spend too much time in the water, you'll find your skin has undergone a change. As you grasp the porcelain side of the bath to pull yourself out, you may notice your fingertips resemble wrinkled old prunes. Water from the bath has soaked into your skin, but in doing so, the water has combined with other molecules in your system, resulting in a liquid that's too big to go back out the way it came—through your skin's pores. You sit there, soaking and bloating and soaking and bloating, until...the water has nowhere else to go but up and out, forcing the skin around your fingertips into new and exciting places. And how do we release this excess water that has caused our dainty digits to look so horrid? Pee, sweat, and tears. Yes, science has proven it: WRINKLED FINGERTIPS ARE GROSS! Bathtime will never be the same again.

Scientist A

Scientist B

What are we doing here, Scientist B?

I think the author wants us to say some sort of good-bye. Do you have anything clever or scientific to say to the readers?

As a scientist, it is my duty to be clever and scientific!

I know. But do you have anything to tell the readers?

Yes! Read the acknowledgments page. It's acknowledge-tastic!

Amazingly Awesome Acknowledgments

I'm just a guy who happens to think weird animals and gross facts are cool. This book wouldn't be possible without the help of some researchers and a lot of very knowledgable experts on all of the subjects you've been reading about. I am forever indebted to the medical consultation of **Tavis J. Basford, BSc**, a man who risked losing his lunch on numerous occasions to ensure that the body facts here are not only gross, but true! And now, please put your hands together in a big round of applause for:

Dr. Ed Bailey, University of Guelph

Raoul Bain, Center for Biodiversity and Conservation, American Museum of Natural History

William E. Barklow, Ph.D., Department of Biology, Framingham State College

Anne Bosy, Fresh Breath Clinic

Tracey K. Brown, Ph.D., California State University, San Marcos

Dr. Howard Burke

Peter E. Busher, Ph.D., Professor of Science, Boston University

Ronald L. Calabrese, Ph.D., Professor of Biology, Emory University

J. Michael Conlon, Ph.D., Department of Biochemistry, United Arab Emirates University

Dr. John R. Conway, Department of Biology, University of Scranton

Gill Diamond, Ph.D., Department of Oral Biology, New Jersey Dental School

Thomas Eisner, Ph.D., Cornell Institute for Research in Chemical Ecology

Dr. Gaetan Faubert, Institute of Parasitology, McGill University

M. Brock Fenton, Ph.D., Professor of Biology, York University

Andrew Fox, Rodney Fox Shark Experience

James H. Harding, Michigan State University

Dr. Jason Hershorn, Optometrist

Joanne Lisa Huber

Nicholas J. Hudson, School of Life Sciences, University of Queensland

Peter G. Kevan, Ph.D., Deptartment of Environmental Biology, University of Guelph

Bill Kohlmoos, President, The Turkey Vulture Society

Joseph G. Kunkel, Ph.D., Professor, University of Massachusetts, Amherst

Dr. Jack L. Littlepage, University of Victoria

Frederic H. Martini, Ph.D., University of Hawaii

Katherine McCarville, Museum of Geology, South Dakota School of Mines

Carl Mehling, Division of Paleontology, American Museum of Natural History

Yona Sipos Randor, University of British Columbia

John G. Robinson, Ph.D., The Wildlife Conservation Society

Bill Saul, Former Collection Manager in Ichthyology, Academy of Natural Sciences, Philadelphia

Catherine Semple, Technical Specialist, Canadian Food Inspection Agency

Dr. Ronald A. Sherman, Department of Pathology, University of California, Irvine

Rob Slotow, School of Life & Environmental Sciences, University of Natal, Durban, South Africa

Atsuko Takamatsu, Ph.D., The University of Tokyo

Dr. Paul Thompson, University of Aberdeen, Lighthouse Field Station

Koen Vandenberghe

Dr. Robert G. White, Professor Emeritus, University of Alaska, Fairbanks

Dr. William F. Wood, Department of Chemistry, Humboldt State University

Answer to page 47: Bromohydrosis means that you've got excess body odor, which means that you stink, and no one wants you near them! Hyperhydrosis is another word for excessive sweating. See how each word has the suffix "hydrosis"? Hydro is the old Greek word for water, which you'll notice leaking out of you when sweating buckets.

Index